FLOWERING LIMBS

FLOWERING LIMBS

STEPHEN KNIGHT

BLOODAXE BOOKS

ISBN: 1 85224 246 9

First published 1993 by
Bloodaxe Books Ltd,
P.O. Box 1SN,
Newcastle upon Tyne NE99 1SN.

Bloodaxe Books Ltd acknowledges
the financial assistance of Northern Arts.

Cover printing by J. Thomson Colour Printers Ltd, Glasgow.

Printed in Great Britain by
Cromwell Press Limited, Broughton Gifford, Melksham, Wiltshire.

For A.S.D. Wright
1959–1987

Acknowledgements

Acknowledgements are due to the editors of the following publications in which some of these poems first appeared: *Encounter, The Honest Ulsterman, London Magazine, London Review of Books, New Statesman, The Observer, Oxford Poetry, Poetry Durham, Poetry Review, Straight Lines, The Times Literary Supplement* and *Verse*; *Against the Grain* (Nelson, 1989), *The Bright Field: Contemporary Poetry from Wales* (Carcanet, 1991), *The Chatto Book of Cabbages and Kings* (1989), *New Poetry 9* (Arts Council/P.E.N./Hutchinson, 1983), *P.E.N. New Poetry II* (Quartet, 1988) and *Poetry Introduction 6* (Faber, 1985).

'The Awkward Age' was a prizewinner in the 1984 National Poetry Competition. A collection including many of these poems received a Gregory Award from the Society of Authors in 1987 – three appeared in *The Gregory Anthology 1987-1990* (Hutchinson, 1990). Seven of these poems were broadcast on BBC Radio 3's *New Voices* in 1991, others on *Poetry Now*.

Thanks to Janet Samuel, aged 11, of Ysgol Gyfun Gŵyr for her essay 'A Fascinating Room'.

Contents

1.

A Species of Idleness

The rise in temperature wakes me now...
The bedclothes gather at my ankles.
Dressing, I check if the street is wet
for the first time in weeks: our window-
box is spiriting away the dregs
from the teapot like a colander.
My bedroom is a pigsty. Last night,
I slept on the ceiling with the moths.

My parents have been anchoring me
to furniture since the Fifth of June –
I spend the afternoons sunbathing
with a weight on my feet. My head still
rises up uncompromisingly.
The neighbours call me 'Dandelion'.
To cool myself, I lay my cheekbones
on our fat refrigerator door.

When a letter from Australia
arrives, it's taken to the kitchen
like a stack of dirty plates: I work
my way through the A4 sheets, clotted
with Tony's spidery hand. *Today,*
he writes, *I recorded the Outback –*
the clicking spokes of a bicycle,
the clack of hockey sticks from a field.

It's a bleak, vernal Sunday; the fish
in the river are counting their scales.
Your typewritten picture-postcards are
as cold as rubber gloves, and yet I
stand them on my desk and mantelpiece.
Have you no time to send a letter?
Food is never off my mind. Weightless
and bored, I feed on every page's

pieces of good advice: how to fill
the vacuum with games of patience
and botany – my hair is growing
faster than the grass (so I settle
for dry shampoo) and the king of clubs
reminds me of my two-faced father!
Despite my thorough shuffling, he
continues floating to the surface.

Every breeze disturbs me. I flicker
with the leaves and the pages of my
writing-pad like fire. Tending to drift,
I fill my pockets with stones and wear
a diver's metal boots, though they clash
with all my clothes. Tony recommends
fresh air and plenty of fruit. My skin
browns like bitten apple in the sun.

Anatomy Class

Like a shiny pendulum, my brother returned home
at regular intervals. One afternoon in May,
he visited with a skeleton; I hadn't seen
his pink face pinker with enthusiasm since he
    pushed a syringe in our mother's upper arm.

The bones were neatly stacked, like cutlery. 'Uterus,'
he murmured, 'liver, kidneys, bladder...,' itemising
absent organs. Our parents – smiling at the mention
    of every piece – continued with the dinner.

I picked my way through the vertebrae, the yellowing
rib cage and the jewellery of her misplaceable
finger bones; our dining-room window faces westward
    and the sunset lit my brother's spectacles.

The skull would make (I remember thinking) a perfect
paper-weight, despite the swastika scratched on the lid.
As we moved to the living-room for tea and eclairs,
my brother packed the set of bones away. Sulkily, I ran
    my finger down the spindly table's leg.

The Top Floor

Our bottled foetus
has flowering limbs,
I close the cupboard door
on it. In his room,
Mister Robins
is folding down
the thumbed corner
of a page of Milton,
loving the solid brickwork
of the verse.
I reach the top floor
panting;
a panatella
turns to dust
between his ochrous fingers.
In the yard, pupils
congregate like spawn:
a group of First Years
debate the size
of Barbra Streisand's breasts.
I lie
flat across the sill
and bellow to my friend
four floors below.
Looking up, he cups
his hands to his ears.
Angelic and bald,
our bottled foetus
wallows in stasis
as vowels and consonants
fall like sediment.

The Bottle of Smoke

Not dust exactly: not exactly wool
coiled behind the glass, inside the neck.
A measure of mist – coalescing, in the cold,
to a complicated knot.
Unlike other clouds, a blue cloud
pushing against the cork
until the cork begins to squeak.
Ghosts of the carpet gathered from the foot
of every wall, of every downstairs wall.
A genie. A storm. A bottle of smoke.

On hands and knees
to check the floorboards for anything missed,
I had my tweezers and a comprehensive list
of things to look for: particles of skin,
a toe- or fingernail, a drawing pin.
I was helping because my eyes were good –
breathing softly, trying not to sneeze,
afraid of losing the pieces I'd gained.
The adults came and went but nothing was explained
all day. It was assumed I understood.

Men plucked light bulbs and curtain hooks
while my mother sorted books:
stopping to smooth the creaky pages:
reading: remembering: tilting her head.
In the emptied room next door,
I straightened up to try the echo,
hooting like a seal then slapping the floor.
Our tall removal men were taking ages.
Their motto, on the side of every lorry, said
'You *Can* Take It With You When You Go'.

I squinted – in the half-light of the inside
of the smaller van – at fifteen
thick-skinned bottles and phials.
(The mouth of every bottle wide enough
to squeeze my torso through.)
One for cobwebs. One for bits of bathroom tiles.
One for crumbs and one for that blue,
unidentifiable fluff
I'd found wherever I had been
that afternoon. Moving like the tide

through every desolate room, I came to Grandad
in the comfy, buttoned armchair like a ship.
Forgotten. Still. Someone had written CLEAN ME
on his brow. This made my parents sad
though not too sad, it seemed, to rave about
our future. They saw our future free of doubt.
Level with my parents' knees, all I could see
was Grandad, drifting on dry land.
One mothball in his mottled hand.
My mother's dusty fingertip.

In Case of Monsters

On the way to bed **a)** Take the staircase
slowly. Note how many steps. Never race
to the landing or try to chase
shadows into corners.

b) Place books and comics under your bed –
The Bible is still a safe bet. **c)** Spread
Sheffield knives two feet from your head.
Polish them first. Ask Dad

nicely and he may sharpen them for you.
d) Always *jump* into bed: monsters queue
behind the valance until dew
curdles on the garden.

e) Face the door before you go to sleep.
Remain like that all night. Use string to keep
yourself in place then **f)** Count sheep
to save strain on the knots.

NB Always have your bed well away
from windows and let the room breathe all day
but never, never when the grey
evenings give way to night.

g) Watch the pattern in your curtains change
to things at sunset altogether strange.
In the silence, they rearrange
their disenfranchised smiles.

When you hear your heartbeat on the pillow
h) Count every thump, and if you don't know
now the number of steps to go
before your blood arrives

i) Check the knives.

The Awkward Age

His diary is packed with non-events –
like March the First *I got up late* and March the Third
My teeth are visibly longer, both my cheeks are furred.
When the eristic charm of female scents

leads me on, I follow it till I'm heard.
He sniffs at the Rive Gauche in my room! – If I say
anything at all to him, he either turns away
or stares at me with his big eyes. He purred

like a car in his bedroom yesterday,
watching television with the curtains drawn. *Hair*
sprouts like hair but quicker. Skin thickens. Claws grow out where
nails were bitten down – I'm quoting from May

the Fourth. He is obsessed with girls: their hair,
their hands, the colour of their eyes... *T. said hullo*
again today – she even smiled! But she wouldn't go
to the cinema with me. C'est la guerre!

He's full of Wordsworth's poetry: like snow,
books gather at the foot of his bed. When I tell
him to tidy his things away, he says he's unwell
or working – he walks to the beach below

the golf links almost every night! The smell
of salt lingers on his trousers and his best tweed
jacket for days. There's no need to go, I say, no need.
(We can't seem to bring him out of his shell.)

I love, he says on June the Tenth, *to feed*
the seagulls till they're nice & fat. They don't take fright
if I look them in the eye. Should I be less polite
& try this trick with girls? Would I succeed?

Frosty looks are bad enough, but he might
stop walking with a stoop for me. *Why can't I be,*
he writes on June the Twenty-Third, *smooth-skinned & sexy?*
We get no peace. He shaves three times a night.

Dinner Time

'Her ten fingers' nine nails
were pointed and painted a leathery red,'
she says without batting an eyelid
then hands me her grandmother's photograph.

'Her room was crawling with cobwebs;
stale, diaphanous curtains; and
fifteen Christs on fifteen crosses –
which put me in mind of a rugby team.

I once stayed all night by her smelly sickbed.'
Lowering her voice, she walks her fingers
along the tablecloth towards a fork –
'And cut her with a knife.

A cut so big,' she says then, like an angler,
holds her insubstantial hands apart.
'Well, she bled pure paraffin.'

Pure paraffin! So a haemorrhage
(I ask her) would amount to arson?
She offers a flickering smile.

The Stepfather

Aftershave, the smell of aftershave
tailing him and claiming every room;
the paintwork tarted up in every room;
his pissing on the toilet seat.

We meet about the house and say 'hullo'
as though there were no walls,
no doors to keep us in.
His two shoes big enough to hold the goldfish;

three gross armchairs, each one
crowned with a mane of beige upholstery;
and flowers, flowers reach from every vase.
His hands as cold as bunches of keys.

We consider bribes, perhaps a dog. He shows me
albums filled with relatives I've never met
waiting, like babies, to be identified.
The terrible noises he makes in the dark.

The Quiet Life

Fearing my reflection, I
have banished mirrors from
our room. 'Do you realise,'
she asks, 'that your face is
wasting?' (Of course I do.) 'And
look, abnormally white!'

We wall ourselves up with old
encyclopaedias:
on ghosts, one entry insists
*An explanation must
be sought in the frame of mind
of the person haunted.*

Suspicious of the other
tenants, we cook and eat
at midnight. Now and then, I
venture to the bathroom
and watch a love-bite move through
mauve to saffron on my

throat, or comb my spiky shoots
of unwashed hair. Every
night, we listen for the sound
of footsteps in the snow
and on the landing carpet –
her bloodless, pretty face

presses to our window like
the moon. Books lie open
on the floor: she steps from Kyd
to Swift as though they were
floes of ice. We have begun
to stack them in the drawers

but still more drift to every
corner of the building.
At dawn, we slide into bed
like a pair of bookmarks.
Being cold, I gravitate
towards her in the dark.

From *The Fascinating Room*

Her bedroom hardening
to a small museum:
stilts of light
breaking the clouds,
freckled with dust
and quietly
rusting the wallpaper;
the mattress and the sheets
rippling with her shape;
the burning bedside lamp...
I log these observations
by repeating them to myself
like the nine times table
or learning quotations.

On the desk,
the shadow of her pencil
deepens, minute by minute,
like a bruise –
she has sharpened it
to within three inches
of nothing. Now, I watch
saliva evaporate
where teeth have cracked
the red paint irreparably.
Her plump handwriting
swims on a sheet of foolscap
capable of cutting skin.
I cut my finger

then run my tongue along
the thin and bloodless crack.
In a dish of liquid sugar,
five dead honey bees
have folded their wings
like hairy full stops.
In the corner, her lemonade
is going flat:
bubbles rise
from the side of the tumbler
to vanish on the surface.
I count them for a while
then turn to her essay.
Floral curtains,

she begins,
frame the window
where six crystal birds
stand on the window-sill.
There, the rays
of the morning sun
make them flash
with an iridescent light.
A family of china rabbits
lives on my bedside table,
under the shelter of the lamp.
Tucked in an alcove
on his bed of moss on the shelf,
my horse's skull grins at me.

Brick on brick, her paragraphs
crumble down the page:
everything her room contains
is falling into place.
And with a tact
her father would admire,
she doesn't mention the tree
pushing up to her –
from the foundations,
through the dining-room –
spreading branches
on her ceiling,
leaning against the sill.
Her carpet peels back from the trunk.

22

In the undergrowth
of scribbles, *I remember,*
she has written,
the warm summer afternoon
when we all went
into the countryside
looking for a sheep's skull
to put with my books.
My brothers have one in their room
and I was envious
for I collect things too.
Instead, I discovered
the horse's skull.
Now they are the envious ones!

And still
not a word of the tree —
how it widens
the hole in her floor
year after year; how branches
twist round the legs of her desk;
how still it is,
being so excluded
from every breeze...
As the sun
fades from the runnels of the trunk,
I rise and listen to the thunder:
like the Twenty-Third Psalm
mumbled in assembly.

Theresa

Theresa let fall her copy of *Harpers & Queen*
and as it struck the ground (among her clothes,
books and several pairs of fat, unfashionable shoes) be-
came a bird: her long nose longer, her slim
arms and fingers wings and golden feathers everywhere.

Her father was dismayed, her mother quite reluctant
to remove the droppings from her cotton sheets.
They informed a priest: he took her silence to imply
apostasy – a thoughtless rebellion.
She sat plump in the middle of the bed. Would not budge.

The trendy priest assumed a pose of concentration –
skewering his clean-shaven chin with an oblong
index finger. Then he blessed her, then he left.
Mother makes Theresa shallow bowls
of lemon tea. Bedside, Daddy delivers bulletins:

'I hang up when your spotty boyfriend telephones...'
'Your mother is mixing gin and Librium...'
'I bought a new, smoke-blue Granada yesterday...'
'Your mother insists on knowing when you fly...'
'The windows have been barred, we cannot let you fall...'

The Vivisectionists

Across the lawn his English neighbour
stretches for the zip along her spine:
a clumsy action pushing out the breasts –
'Clumsy, but I like her pointed breasts.'

She wriggles out of her lemon dress,
uncaps a tube of viscous tanning cream
then smooths her warm and auburn body
like a fly polishing six legs clean.

He lives below her room. On Saturdays
she relaxes with her stereo:
Prélude à 'L'Après-midi d'un faune'
floats from her open window like smoke;

he brings up to date his diary's
entries on the colour of her skin...
Last night, he wrote 'A noise on the tiles
outside. She's walking down the wall to me.'

For the Spring Term

Snow, with its own particular silence,
fold over fold, smothers the open roads.
Through the night, breath hardens on the windows.

The bedclothes crush me with feathers.

I think of you driving to Bristol
(your textbooks and cases packed in the boot)
and settle for postcards again –

my close handwriting fills them like footprints,
turning the white into slush!

Your birthday present
– a turquoise mohair sweater –
blossoms at the tips of my mother's needles.

She's fretting about the measurements
but still it drifts towards completion.

While the sun does next to nothing,
I scrape ice from the paths; and now,
I'm toasting your absence

with a glass of water.

The Reproductive Organs

I miss every part of you:
your toes – so long they might
be fingers – and your teeth!

though your handwriting grows
as fast and bulbous as a frog.
It crowds the letters you send.

Having lost track of the days
his mind is a deep, blank stream
of numbers and sentences.

Her envelopes arriving
with second class postage
clang in his head like rust

until *Gradually, silently,*
I become sexless – losing
hair, muscle, genitals.

With a cruel symmetry
his letters multiply while hers
decrease to a dribble.

Forgetful now, she's posting
views of other places
in monochrome and in the snow.

As the webbing on my hands,
he writes, *develops*
day after day, I find it

somewhat difficult to hold
this fountain pen: gills grow where
last you bit my neck. I'll send

a recent photograph.

When the Summer Goes Up in Flames

Men smoke three storeys above your parting,
capitalising on the sunshine –
brick and slate take root in the garden.
The landlord arrives with his landscaped,
baldy hairstyle and we complain about
the noise. Skips become a fitment.

To those events of 1986
recognised in Special Issue stamps
– Halley's Comet, the Commonwealth Games –
we add the growing row over sanctions
and the tufts of grass on your back.

The grass on your back and buttocks tickles
in bed, where we weigh the pros and cons
for scorching. (Zico shimmers through Poles
in the heat of Guadalajara:
a shadow of his former self, he vies
for air-time with Desmond Tutu.)

During downpours, of course, you rush inside
and watch the box; men rattle the planks
above us: *we* try horticulture.
When, arms outstretched at night, the spiders come
to you, scorching crops up again.

Pulling a blade across my lips, between
my teeth, burns the skin: despite a speech
impediment, I'm whingeing about
your chlorophyll – it messes the sheets.
When I roam the length of your naked spine,
green tongues leap between my fingers.

Down among the rubble, the sun that cooks
my shoulders salmon-pink turns your field
to gold. Still tender, you embrace me
gingerly: stiff with calamine, I scrape
your flattened palms like a statue.

The scaffolding goes and I catch myself
staring at my empty hands, missing
ladders and pulleys; the langorous,
autumnal drift of paper falling
to the garden; and talk, idle talk – that
most peculiar of vapours.

The Gift

My parcel was delivered to the college
thoroughly packaged, like an only child.
I tear my father's beautifully-written note
(Please acknowledge receipt, Love Mam & Dad)
then fold the wrapping for possible re-use.
A breeze laps the posters crusting the wall;
like lily pads, they compete to face the light.

I bump into Philip inside the Lodge.
He asks to see the gift – another four-sleeved
pullover! Raising it shoulder-high,
he teases me about the additional arms
till I make my excuses and leave him
at the pigeonholes to scurry to my room.

I lay the jumper on my coverlet
and step back to survey the lively design –
summery shades of green and blue in bars
a centimetre wide around the middle;
and seagulls, too. Trying it on
before my full-length mirror, I turn in circles
like a weather-vane. The sleeves rotate with me!

Dizzier than Lewis Carroll's Alice,
I finish instead an essay due at six...
My sides itch as I write. Just below the ribs,
above my pelvis, carpal bones, knuckles
and ten fingernails push through the flesh like roots.
Should I telephone home, or should I wait?

Towards a Definition of Heaven

I watch the whole house watching me: eight solid rooms.
Here is our deep blue living-room carpet,
lapping the skirting board with threads. His photographs are up.
I sink in the sofa; its concave cushions
hold their dusty breath a little tighter for me.

An unread column of library books
trembles like a fish when I turn the television down.
Faces bob across the screen, buoyed up by pairs of
grey, substantial shoulders. Last week, he was balanced
on the edge of his chair to catch the punchlines.

Today, now, his trousers and his best white shirt
swoon beside the castors. On the antimacassar,
slivers of him coagulate; slower, by far, than grease.
The weather forecast is on: his all-time favourite,
you tell me as you pour the coffee.

As intangible as isobars and swimming in
soft focus, your portrait looks reproachfully
on us – on you rationing me to a level teaspoon
of sugar. I inherit his sweet-tooth,
his books and his recipe for making wine.

Seeing the splashes on your tipsy rubber plant,
I recollect our telephone conversation:
his goitre, you still insist, dripped through his collar;
a tear streamed; and then his whole face streamed; his vital organs
beached on the rug when he hit the blue,

blunt carpet head-first, splashing, yes, the rubber plant...
We'll wipe these incrustations off this afternoon,
before the sun slants in to gild what's left of him.
(I think of a pink meniscus now: chattering with heat
and light and dust; tense before it falls.)

What to Say When You Talk to Yourself

In the corner, doubled up, black PVC,
my travelling bag: my four cream walls: my single key:
my wardrobe: my mirror: my coloured underwear:
my sponge bag: my dirty laundry watching me:
my comb, my gel and my spikes of hair:

my box of matches: my sparks:
my wallet and my BR clerks:
my grilles: my Standard Class return
to Paddington: my black remarks:
my fondness for watching things burn:

my rainy pavements, all night
barnacled with yellow light:
my nostalgia for the beach:
my empty rooms: my long sight
and my skinny, boxer's reach:

my arrivals: my departures: my grey, wax-faced
commuters on the Circle Line: my sense of waste:
my animosities: my lungs: my sliding door
hiccuping at Swindon: my freshly-soled and -laced
black boots, fit for pacing my bedroom floor,

and one brittle rose
sandwiched in the prose
of Jonathan Swift:
my forehead, my nose,
my ears and my gift

for hanging pictures well: my rigid way with words:
my desserts: my tasteless ties: my love of birds
with Paxo: big eyes and lips: my skew-whiff smile
dying on my face: my dark, unbroken turds
slipped into the water like a crocodile.

2.

Notes for a Poem Called 'Me Me Me'

When winds from the sea peel back the beach
  A wind from the sea tears down the beach

I'm trying
sentences
and phrases
in my head
Drifting off
thinking of
somewhere
Some things
never change

                eyes and ears of sand
                    years of sand

In autumn, when winds assail the coast, sand reshapes
the dual carriageway: the grains abrade each tree
and every wall that faces out to sea:
dunes billow at the kerb: sand drapes
itself in grey, restless folds
on the empty roads

            *

Wild Frost? Coral Cloud? Or Mulberry Crush?
Your lipstick smudged on a tissue in my fist.

Apart from the ticking of the windscreen wipers,
your car is a fishtank filled with silence

till 'Everyone is well
but the wheels are out of alignment'.

Li's Garden is awash with drunks.
The muscles of your face have frozen shut.

While seagulls crap on the Crazy Golf Course,
the coast-line is blurred by advancing sand.

34

The trickle begins
'I hope that you're established
before I close my eyes for good'

at the promenade,
where the cenotaph runs with green.
My bag on the back seat slides from side to side.

Splashing
the dashboard, your voice is repeating
'Why did we move?...' 'We can never go back...'

The drive
from the station takes twenty minutes.
I smile like a synchronised swimmer...

*

In the corners of rooms
   and in the cupboards of those rooms

furniture is piling up like photographs
   a houseful in a flat

nudging you both
   with the past

dried flowers, heads down, tied at the ankles
   hanging from the curtain rails

the plants that overflow their pots
   dragging their feet across the floor

the thick-set, whingeing drawer
   the tasselled lamp

and everywhere I look, a different clock
   the years of sand between us now

*

The wearing of flippers indoors
   is not allowed

On the carpets/of this flat/I knocked/against my father/like
a cloud

*

                                    'Look,
I don't want to argue, we don't see
that much of you now.'

                      'I know.'

'We just want to see you settled down.
I don't like to think of you wasting
your life in that awful bedsit.
You know we worry.'

                      'I know.'

'You wouldn't be working with dead things.
It's a good job.'

                'Oh yes, very fulfilling –
dusting fossils and mopping up
after school-parties.'

                      'There's more to life
than "Me Me Me".'

                      'I know.'

'We want something better for you –
you know you can't depend
on us forever...'

                      *

My room is a tunnel on the first floor:
the door at one end; a sink; a table;
the bed; then a window at the other.

The building hoards shadows through the summer
to hold them on my nostrils, mouth and eyes.
The smells of other tenants crowd the air.

Sharing the bathroom opposite my door
I discover trails of liquid footprints
and wafers of soap thin enough to post.

A soupçon of pubic hairs (three or four)
crops up in the tub, below the halo
of dirt. I have bought a bottle of Jif.

Buff envelopes from the DHSS
accumulate on the hallway table
beside the pay-phone, in the dark, like rice.

The ground floor kitchen bubbles with voices.
The cooker in the corner runs on gas.
The oven, at a pinch, can hold three heads.

*

I'm trying sentences and phrases in my head

*

Potatoes in the wardrobe
release their shoots
towards the light –
reaching beyond the comics,
the records and the old clothes
hardened in their creases;
or tomatoes on the sill
ripen in the time
it takes to argue.
With muddy tights,
black fingernails and cuts
crusted with blood,
the visits began at Easter:
you rose with your palm
on the small of your back,
you gathered stones
until your cheeks turned red,
until it rained.
The steel drum by the lean-to
filled with rain.

Bumps clustered on the hand
you dipped into nettles
distorted my telephone number...
That weekend, I watched them
subside.

*

With stacks of amber newspapers spilling across the floor
like bricks, my bedroom is a cupboard:
my clothes have hardened in their folds,
the shapes of me at seventeen

        where shadows thicken to spiders

*

The need to provide never goes:
sometimes underpants, usually socks.

*

The Sundays I leave, more often than not
(and whether I ask you to help me

or not) my bag is packed for the journey
then placed among the cardboard boxes

1 sponge cake dusty with sugar
2 lbs of runner beans
a half-eaten packet of peanuts
an armful of new potatoes
1 lettuce   4 leeks
a box of paper handkerchiefs
my washed and ironed shirts

and the strap cutting into my shoulder
from here, to the train, to the house

where

*

Sunday morning, the three of us out for a drive. Nursing the suspension, you ease the car along a pot-holed road to Sandy Lane, to the house where you first made a home together thirty-five years ago. Occasionally, I lurch to one side in the back seat, putting out a hand to steady myself.

I say 'house' but 'shack' would be more appropriate: *Golf View* is a beach hut built on the edge of Pennard links. In the photographs we have, my brother – who must be under five – sits on a tricycle on the veranda, staring into the lens. My grandparents look benignly down at him. Since then, the veranda has been enclosed and my brother's eyes are not as blue.

On the short walk there, you remark on the changes since 1953. Surprisingly few, it seems. Several huts have been cleared and there are circles of scorched earth through which, I like to believe, blades of grass will push. A pair of goats are tethered to a gatepost and there's a dog imprisoned in a makeshift garden. 'Write a poem about this,' my father suggests awkwardly. Poetry embarrasses him.

We talk about an odd mixture of subjects; mostly things arising from our visit. Mortgages, for one; and past mistakes. There are crumbs of information about my father's parents: how they lost everything in the Depression – sold their silver, their furniture, everything – and moved to London, where my father grew up. In later years, my grandmother would point out the house in Swansea where she knew her sideboard was.

Peering through the window of *Golf View* you think you recognise a mirror. If anything does come back to you, standing before that bright green shack with the glass-paper roof, you keep it to yourselves. You are, both of you, ageing like sand. I barely remember your profiles.

We leave, lurching back the way we came. It's autumn and things are going to sleep. I put out a hand to steady myself.

*

Overlooking
the sounds of the sea

at the bottom
of Mary Twill Lane

the whitewashed
Home For The Blind

is hard to the touch
all year round

The clocks
are turned back in October

Winter
is a cleaner smell

The pier and lighthouse
stammer all night

for tankers
moaning in the bay

like ghosts
like the Braille warning

stamped
on a bottle of bleach

*

The winds are fogged with dirt,
the trees and sky becoming black & white

colour is out of reach

*

Two pictures and a mirror/adrift from the wall, adrift from
their nails

The grandchildren grow around the room –
a disconnected sequence of faces thinning
towards adolescence; smiling with one
and then another
set of teeth

        the chewed end of a pencil
        trousers stiff with paint

Too high to clean, the windows are fogged with dirt.

Light tangles in the overcast net–curtain
or submerges in the sofa's whorls.

Crammed in the flat on bended knees, my father
measures for shelves – your houseful of furniture
hugs the walls of all four rooms like moss
and every room is a maze of boxes
rearranged before my weekends home.

The middle of the night is unfamiliar.

Squinting at his pencil marks, he talks about
the Ganges Delta; heat; his war at a wireless
receiving coded messages –
dots and dashes drummed in his ears
while his hands worked automatically.
He thought of home. He thought of rain…

When the nails and screws are put aside like sweets
and the brushes loll in a jar of milky turps,
two shelves list in their coats of paint.

Glasses, china tigers and a wooden mule from Spain
play Grandmother's Footsteps towards the beaded edge
…

        sentences and phrases
        slip to the edge of the world

*

Although you didn't have
to take me to the station
nor stay until the train
pulled out of sight
you did
      so I waved as I went
like royalty
        and now
I crane towards that window
wondering how far I've gone,
how far I have
to go –
      I see nothing
but a string of lights
and the hollows of my face
scooped out by the night.
Overhead, my bag's as plump
as a cartoon thundercloud.

I was meaning to ask
– but there wasn't the time –
why so many boxes
remain unpacked
or why your long aquarium
is overgrown and murky.
More silt than fish
whenever I looked.

(Those crumbs of food
untouched on the surface.
That permanent
           aposiopesis
of bubbles...
        The flick
of a tail
     in the dark)

       *

         the gravel meadows

3.

On the Edge of Monday Morning

Against the wall, like a square of chocolate,

the storage heater snores through the small hours:

heat blossoms from every pore, curling round

the tendrils of the television set.

Two storeys up, the potted plants look out

of place. Last night is melting on the pane.

In the broad-leafed shadows, my mother wakes.

Five blind fingers go feeling for the light.

Dream Kitchen

Envelopes wait by the door like sunsets.
Uncollected in a fortnight,
they shout through their cellophane windows

Congratulations, Miss Collister
you've been specially chosen
Before the landlord sends them back

they swim among the leaflets
and the telephone directories, in the hall,
where the timer turns the light off prematurely.

Three Tenancy Agreements later, the room
where Miss Collister lived is white again
and The Occupant is pregnant.

Pushing fingers through her wavy hair
like dolphins, she watches crumpled paper
open in the corner of that room:

In fifteen words or less – Living in London
without a Kenwood Chef is bearable because
IN MY REVERIES, WE ALL RECEIVE THE LETTERS WE WANT

The Eyeball Works

Ad-men bandy slogans, like *PUPILS GUARANTEED...*
The would-be donors queue all afternoon
while tinted windows of The Eyeball Works run cloud
and passer-by at half their normal speed.
Into the evening, noises draw a crowd –
footsteps on a flight of marble stairs;
murmurs from an unlit foyer and the slow,
self-satisfied give of drapery and armchairs
laundered to the colour of the moon.
Noses flatten on the glass like dough.

Inside, the Eyeball Brochures packed in crates
whiff, unmistakably, of Money and Success;
they leave from the dock doors every night
with details of bargains and sell-by dates.
The workers, clothed in dust-revealing white,
wear gloves that cling and oblong paper hats,
each stamped with a Happy Eyebrows trademark.
For safety's sake, they stand on rubber mats –
before their lightly-greased machines – to press,
drill, gouge and slice until it's dark.

The marble benches are cobbled with eyes
arranged in rows then opened like books;
eyes jostle in dishes, eyes bob in jars
labelled according to status and size.
Eyes for Librarians and *Eyes of the Stars*
anticipate one of those numerous tinges
(from Palimpsest Azure to Paul Newman Blue)
stored in carboys, doled out through syringes.
Every jar is packed with long, blank looks
and the needles are true.

Tonight, Security is a humming sound
and the smell of disinfectant damp on floors.
Tonight, the door knobs are electrified
and the ugly dog let loose in the compound
pads down corridors like a bride...
Small cameras on the ceilings wink and weave
while, tapping the walls with his complimentary stick,
the last of the donors to leave
is 'leaving' through the NO ADMITTANCE doors.
He waves Goodbye. The doors go tick, tick, tick.

The Summer with Uncle Günther

Living in a bricks-and-mortar wedding cake,
he cultivates The Gigolo's thin moustache.
The doors; the furniture; the skirting board
piped around the walls; the walls – everything is white
and friable. Our shoes remain on the porch.

In stockinged feet (to save the carpets) I pass
from room to room. Ornaments accrue like ash
from Italy and Greece: a plaster negress
and satyrs with dubious, curved erections
standing in gangs on the cabinets.

My cousin visits twice a month. We settle
in the cool, dark lounge to gulp our squash
and play Monopoly. Sometimes we burrow
to the heart of the house, where the wasps collapse,
to watch her father dyeing his temples black.

'Uncle' Vincent

One week later the door was broken down
and he was there, sitting to attention –
an ex-ballet dancer, fifty-four years
of age, your adopted uncle, dead man.

He left an inscription on the flyleaf
of your dictionary: *1974.*
To Katie. You may not appreciate
this gift at the moment, by Ten you will.

Surrounded by shelves of his souvenirs
in a rented room, he closed his eyes:
Cliff Richard posters beaming down at him:
motes thickening like words on his treasure.

Treasure. Noun. Accumulated wealth,
gems or precious metals or a hoard of them,
valued thing, darling or useful person.
(And in his careful hand, he spelt your name wrong.)

Voyage to the Bottom of the Sea

The trick (he tells me) is to sleep till twelve
    then watch the television.
In the corner of his murky bedroom
    there is always a swirl of colour:

T-shirts; smoke threading from an ashtray
    to the light; shoes; anemones thriving
on the wreck of the Torrey Canyon;
    our Chancellor raising the Budget box.

The Body-Parts Launderette
(for Sacha Brooks)

Four legs go in: the headboard's next: it's grey,
it's cold where a birdcage and a bed in sections
furnish the space outside The Last Chance antique shop.
At sundown, in the launderette, every day
long, neon striplights twitch into life –
light spills across the pavement like a knife.
Windows mist. Shapes move inside and the evenings drag.
The sounds of agitation never stop.
Stuffed with handbills or copies of the local rag,
the letterbox is down at ankle-height.
Footprints lead away in all directions.
The Body-Parts Launderette is open through the night.

In the window, cards and leaflets face the street
like ghosts: the Car Boot Sale that came and went; masseurs
without surnames; *RADIOS FOR SALE*; School Fêtes.
When the ancient machinery shivers and purrs,
puddles appear from cracks in the concrete floor
then seep towards strategically-placed, steel grates.
There's a pay-phone; a bin; a woman's calf
and the patron saint of The Body-Parts Launderette,
Dennis Nilsen, watching from a photograph
nailed to the Supervisor's padlocked, metal door.
One laundry basket's filled with odd feet
customers have left behind. It's dripping wet.

The Supervisor, for her sins, wears
fluffy mules and a quilted dressing-gown.
She burnishes the hacksaws, chains and knives
hung from the yellowing walls; or gathers up
the ticked and folded questionnaires
that quiz the customers about their empty lives.
Have you used 1) *An acid bought in town*
2) *Soap, or* 3) *Detergent in a paper cup?*
Somewhere between a coma and a dream,
alone, on plastic seats, they pass whole days
in front of tedious machines; watching the steam,
the suds, those churning reds and greys.

The Body Politic

Sam Knight, the Weights & Measures man,
   bequeaths the softer pieces of himself
to medical research: bits and bobs
   go with as little fuss as breath on glass.

His room at the Guest House is let within days.
   At the window – faced with bony children
picking bottles off the shore – his bust of Lenin
   leaves a clean square on the sill.

Confetti
(for Katy)

Dead leaves cross the threshold and the owner knows.
Arriving in a red Mercedes frilled with rust

an hour before the newlyweds, he cleans the hall,

the stairs, Flat 3; I am keeping quiet
while the hoover snuffles around our door.

There is little to show you this evening:
a line, perhaps, that starts but doesn't finish

and my face, white enough to scribble on.

I am eating my biro, keeping quiet
while transactions finish in the room above.

Testy, tired from school, you'll crash in on this,
my own Gorillagram! Kicking off your shoes,

squatting on the sofa to cleanse your face with Ten-O-Six!

When you litter the floor with buds of cotton wool
black from the dirt of your day,

The Arts Council/Theatre Club Coffin Annexe
(for Seona McKinnon)

Old themselves, our usherettes begin to cry
when the audience arrives, in twos and threes;
fifty at most, in beds, in wheelchairs, with nurses
and legatees. Wraiths of the theatre's past.
Meanwhile, backstage, mention of the curse is
frightening the Thane of Glamis. Down on his knees
in Dressing Room 1, he runs his soliloquies
under his breath. Those members of the cast
who double-up prepare to die: to live: to die.
This Autumn Season will be the last.

Apart from the still of a pre-war Farce
– martinis, cigarettes and slicked-back hair –
the walls of the foyer are totally bare.
That single concession's a drawing pin short.
It curls in (imperceptibly, as cripples pass)
like a breaker; and nobody seems to care.
The Box Office matron is moving her lips,
leaning towards the small hole in the glass
for air. When her words emerge in drips,
the deaf-aids whistle and snort.

The backstage tannoy has fizzled awake.
Beginners. In the twilight, in the wings,
Duncan rolls his head; his fingers shake
and the office is empty. Blacks hang on the door.
Production schedules itemise the days before –
the Tech, each Dress; each moment, every break
laid out like a will then pinned on the board.
Somewhere down the corridor, someone sings
New York, New York softly. Waves breaking on the shore.
Like the wish for somewhere else, somewhere unexplored.

The Coffin Annexe is unlocked for the night;
one icy room we fill to the roof
with the help of an Arts Council grant.
Nailed shut, or snug as Russian dolls; upright
in pairs, like cruets; alone and on a slant
leaning against the bare-bricked, Annexe wall
they wait, for a week at most. Out of sight...
And now, superior, distant, aloof,
the DSM is repeating her latest call.
The play arrives in whispers. Whispers rise and fall.

The Band Room next door is a history book.
The crew relax, among the props, before the Half
here, where the past is wherever they look;
and this is what's left of the dated and the dead.
The goose in a black & white photograph –
funny legs and feathers blurred when the camera shook.
Loose-leafed scripts, each title page curling like bread.
Warm to the touch, stained with dregs,
a teacup balanced on the Giant's paper head.
The last of those insurmountable, golden eggs.

The Silent Chair

With its tongue removed, the bell above the door
shook like dust as we stepped inside The Silent Chair.
The menu listed prices from the year before.
The RNLI box was filled with air.

Splayed on the walls, a clutch of Chinese fans
grew cooking fat while the sign among them roared
THE MANAGEMENT REQUIRES YOU DO NOT USE YOUR VOICE
No words! No sounds! Nothing audible permitted
though when it came to soup, the blackboard
on the counter was powdery with choice –

tomato   mulligatawny   pea   shark's fin
Our drifting waitress arrived with the faintest of tans
and, wide across her mouth, that band of white skin
where a gag had been fitted.

In from the rain, unused to speaking anyway,
the clientele was muffled with beards and coats.
They kept to themselves and passed the time
ordering tea with a simple mime –
twisting their wrists or stroking their throats.
I don't know now if there was anything to say

but why, of all things, should I still recall
the tables pushed apart like single beds?
The shark's fin soup? Or the clock on the wall
dripping on our stupid, stupid, stupid heads?

The Diving Board
Pennsylvania

As Achilles lolls beside the pool
in dappled Bermuda shorts, he sips
gin and orange from a tumbler
and strums the water's tuneless surface
with a pilose, tanned paw. Fish gather.

His white, athletic wife is bouncing
on the diving board. Two face-lifts old,
her skin is stretched like canvas
on a frame of unexceptional bone:
a picture of health by Picasso.

His stationary manner annoys her,
she hectors him and keeps herself trim
with aerobics. Achilles has laced
the deep end with barracuda, he
believes in living dangerously.

The Wig Replacement Clinic

Sandstone; gargoyles; bricked-up windows; and a window
that looks onto Wind Street, where the prostitutes go.
The Clinic is rotting on the darker edge
of town – it borders waste ground set aside
for a car park then forgotten. Now winos make fires.
Burning prams. Burning tyres.
When storm clouds trundle in with the tide,
seagulls and pigeons drop to a favoured ledge,
old posters flutter on the Clinic's shitty walls
and the temperature falls.

The window display is furry with dust –
dust builds on the posters of Paradise
(four views of Fiji); on the hanging plants that rust
through lack of water; on every wig and on the price
of every wig. 'Salvation is at hand,'
the window whispers, 'Come to me.'
Customers pause at a small, brass plaque
to check their hair, to dab each wayward strand.
THE WIG REPLACEMENT CLINIC plc
and the black sky crackles like a heart attack.

Beyond the famous door, double doors
flap shut with a squawk and the lobby is dim
and echoing. A smell of cupboards, of empty drawers.
The photographs mounted on the walls are grim
but Happy Customers, grey behind the glass –
each right-hand corner is signed
like a cheque. The furnishing is sparse:
a laughably-small reception desk; two rows
of chairs (the bony, uncomfortable kind)
and a clock that no longer goes.

At the far end of the corridor
there's a hatstand rooted to the parquet floor.
The Receptionist's repeated yawning has begun
to fog her afternoon. It's later than she supposes.
Counting off the working weeks, she longs for sun
and, by the single light bulb, reads her book.
(Romances, reams of hairy chests and roses,
are tunnelled through at the rate of one a day.)
She never gives the balding men a second look.
Hardened? Tactful? Bored? She doesn't say.

She waves her bookmark at a wonky chair
or mumbles 'Doctor T—— ' (or K—— , or X——) 'is
ready to see you now.' Her smile is not quite there.
If the *Reader's Digest* has gone, the wall
includes a few celebrities – both sexes,
old and young – to recognise. Their broad grins appal.
From somewhere overhead, there's the hum
of large machinery; far off, almost dental.
Sometimes other noises come:
human noises: patients being 'temperamental'.

Beyond the hatstand is a staircase
coiling, drifting upwards; wider than the span
of three men with their arms extended – fingertips
to fingertips – its upper reaches vanish into space.
The banister is cambered and thick:
mahogany python. Heels boom. Stilettos click.
Adjusting to the gloom, a patient comes to grips
with the building's floor-by-floor plan:
the rooms are numbered but the key to 'what' and 'where'
is missing, or was never there.

The noises from rooms arrive at the stairwell,
pause, cut loose then fall with a clatter.
Coughing. Whispers. Drilling. Sounds that barely matter...
The first flight cripples the legs and the heart.
There's an axe, on the landing, in a red box
labelled FIRE. – Should a blaze ever start,
the doors would prove too solid, the locks
too intricate. Light streams from the fish–eye
set above each number. Pins and needles. Slivers of sky.
Each door has a small, fluorescent button labelled BELL.

The hinges are clean and padded with oil.
Unlocked, unbolted, each door unfolds like a feather.
Then light: white light roaring out: furnace light in one go
breaking on the customer: marble: polar bear: snow...
Focus on the fitments, plump with skin-brown leather.
From a tall, discreetly-placed machine, cables coil
towards the corner, where they meet.
Hooks grow from the walls and on them, rugs;
wigs; waterproof toupees, half-finished or complete.
The desk is stacked with jars of drugs.

Above the peeling couch, posters and charts
cling onto Blu-Tack: bird's-eye views of the head;
diagrams of follicles apparently dead;
maps of barren lands; and where the hard sell starts
with pictures of men looking sadder, older,
there's a bevy of Kitemarks and Union Jacks
to inspire hubris – something the customer lacks.
The jars are shivering, shoulder to shoulder,
pills rumble and jump. Behind the screens
in every room, vibrations ripple from big machines.

The cow-eyed, hopeless patients are aware
(albeit dimly as they touch their falling hair)
of a movement beneath their feet
that shakes the furniture; a steady heartbeat.
Shrunken in their clothes, they sit in corners
of those rooms, touching their faces like mourners.
No breaking glass, no noise, no smell, no mess
of brick and plaster could compete with their distress.
They struggle to control their breath. They stare.
Fingers numb, palms up, they hold their fallen hair.

In every whitewashed room, the catalogue
of sadness is repeated: crumpled faces,
crumpled clothes, alopecia in a thousand forms.
And when they leave, tears fill the echoing spaces.
Dark glasses help; a trilby disguises and warms;
when a toupee wears a client down the corridor, eyes clog.
Through the lobby they go, past the grey Receptionist
who doesn't glance up from her book but prays
for sun! Escape! The chance of being kissed!
In The Wig Replacement Clinic, winter stays.

Outside, the redistribution of dirt begins
with bits of soggy cardboard flushed from bins.
Umbrellas mushroom and the doorways of shops
run with brown-water footprints. Rain drops
on the Clinic like dust. Rain smears.
When the last one out pulls shut the famous door
then steps into the night, it's late.
He folds his hair behind his ears:
his head a little higher than before:
that beatific kiss-curl melting on his pate.

Apogee of the Infamous Carnival Killer

Autumn. Dusk. It's the end of the season
and punters are thin on the ground.
Also thin on the hardened ground is Ginger,
the Elastic Man, garrotted by the flex of a two-pin plug.
A Detective Constable chalks around the corpse;
distracted, he conjures up
the fleshy contours of his wife.

The freaks in the Big Top – hardly 'Big' –
cry softly for Ginger: the Bearded Lady
dabbing her button nose with a Kleenex;
Samson consoling the Fat Lady (he cannot
stretch his arm around her shoulders, she's crying
buckets for her friend); and the bogus Tattooed Man
dissolving shamelessly.

Inside his cage, the Man Beast rattles the bars
for show: gentle as a leveret,
he is above suspicion.
While the freaks are swapping memories, alibis
and stunts for the following night, Ginger
is stretchered away. Metres above him, the Fly-
ing Zantini tumble into nothing.

Double Writing

Sea View, Water's Edge, Atlantis,
lugubrious Guest Houses welcome the tide

after dark, from the opposite side of the road.
Their windows are lit with VACANCIES.

At closing time, Covelli's chips do a roaring trade
though his name has flaked from the side of the building.

Tighter than fists in the gaps in wooden benches,
pages of the local paper soak in vinegar.

Wind sizzles through trees
while, from the promenade, waves reach for the last bus

back into town. Ticking over in the back seat,
somebody sleeps it off. His thumb is in his mouth.

The timetable never works
and graffiti spreads through the shelter like wires –

refinements of a thick, black autograph
above the spray of glass, below the one-armed clock.

In West Cross garages, drums, guitars and microphones
huddle together, waiting to be famous.

Things go quiet. Things are unplugged.
Cutlery is laid out for the morning.

Blue Skies

Following every storm
old photographs emerged like wings
from the bedroom, though nothing
could restore the calm

of years before, before they came to any harm –
turn-ups, a polka dot dress, one blustery day;
her arm hooked round his arm
as if that could stop him blowing away.